M000039228

Greater Than a Tourist
Book Series
Reviews from Readers

I think the series is wonderful and beneficial for tourists to get information before visiting the city.

-Seckin Zumbul, Izmir Turkey

I am a world traveler who has read many trip guides but this one really made a difference for me. I would call it a heartfelt creation of a local guide expert instead of just a guide.

-Susy, Isla Holbox, Mexico

New to the area like me, this is a must have!

 -Joe, Bloomington, USA

This is a good series that gets down to it when looking for things to do at your destination without having to read a novel for just a few ideas.

-Rachel, Monterey, USA

Good information to have to plan my trip to this destination.

-Pennie Farrell, Mexico

Great ideas for a port day.

-Mary Martin USA

Aptly titled, you won't just be a tourist after reading this book. You'll be greater than a tourist!

-Alan Warner, Grand Rapids, USA

Even though I only have three days to spend in San Miguel in an upcoming visit, I will use the author's suggestions to guide some of my time there. An easy read - with chapters named to guide me in directions I want to go.

 -Robert Catapano, USA

Great insights from a local perspective! Useful information and a very good value!

 -Sarah, USA

This series provides an in-depth experience through the eyes of a local. Reading these series will help you to travel the city in with confidence and it'll make your journey a unique one.

-Andrew Teoh, Ipoh, Malaysia

GREATER THAN A TOURIST- NEPAL

50 Travel Tips from a Local

Anand Dhakal

Cover designed by: Ivana Stamenkovic
Cover Image: https://pixabay.com/photos/himalayas-ama-dablam-mountain-
nepal-409/

CZYK Publishing Since 2011.

Greater Than a Tourist

Lock Haven, PA
All rights reserved.

ISBN: 9781692753306

>TOURIST

50 TRAVEL TIPS FROM A LOCAL

BOOK DESCRIPTION

Are you excited about planning your next trip? Do you want to try something new? Would you like some guidance from a local? If you answered yes to any of these questions, then this Greater Than a Tourist book is for you. *Greater Than a Tourist- Nepal* by Anand Dhakal gives you the inside scoop on Nepal. Most travel books tell you how to travel like a tourist. Although there is nothing wrong with that, as part of the Greater Than a Tourist series, this book will give you travel tips from someone who has lived at your next travel destination.

In these pages, you will discover advice that will help you throughout your stay. This book will not tell you exact addresses or store hours but instead will give you excitement and knowledge from a local that you may not find in other smaller print travel books.

Travel like a local. Slow down, stay in one place, and get to know the people and culture. By the time you finish this book, you will be eager and prepared to travel to your next destination.

Inside this travel guide book you will find:

- Insider tips from a local.

- Packing and planning list.

- List of travel questions to ask yourself or others while traveling.

- A place to write your travel bucket list.

OUR STORY

Traveling is a passion of the Greater than a Tourist book series creator. Lisa studied abroad in college, and for their honeymoon Lisa and her husband toured Europe. During her travels to Malta, an older man tried to give her some advice based on his own experience living on the island since he was a young boy. She was not sure if she should talk to the stranger but was interested in his advice. When traveling to some places she was wary to talk to locals because she was afraid that they weren't being genuine. Through her travels, Lisa learned how much locals had to share with tourists. Lisa created the Greater Than a Tourist book series to help connect people with locals. A topic that locals are very passionate about sharing.

TABLE OF CONTENTS

14. Don't Miss visiting Garden of Dreams:

15. Enjoy Stunning Views From Nagarkot:

16. Visit Hanuman Dhoka:

17. Say 'Namaste' While Greeting Nepalese People:

18. Roam In The Street Of Thamel:

19. Visit Casino Royale:

20. Explore Kumari Bahal:

21. Visit Central Zoo:

22. See The Remains Of Dharahara:

23. Travel To Pokhara:

24. Stay In The Lakeside:

25. Visit Phewa Tal (Lake):

26. Visit Rupa Tal:

27. Visit Sarangkot:

28. Visit Gorkha Memorial Museum:

29. Enjoy In Davi's fall:

30. Visit The Annapurna Butterfly Museum:

31. Travel To Chitwan:

32. Visit Chitwan National Park:

33. Go To Chitwan Tharu Village:

34. Canoeing In Narayani River:

35. Enjoy Elephant Safari:

36. Explore Elephant Breeding Center:

37. Enjoy Elephant Bathing:

38. Visit The Crocodile Breeding Center:

DEDICATION

This book is dedicated to all the tourists who are planning to visit Nepal for enjoying their vacation. I have mentioned 50 important travel tips plus two bonus tips for you guys to travel like a local in Nepal. As Nepal is celebrating 'Visit Nepal 2020', I would like to welcome every tourist across the world. Heaven is a myth, but Nepal is real.

ABOUT THE AUTHOR

Anand Dhakal is a Nepalese citizen who lives in the city 'Biratnagar'. He is a supervisor in a private corporation. He is also a great writer, translator, and transcriptionist.

He loves traveling and writing. He had traveled all the tourist destination places of his own country. He found that his country is rich in natural beauties, unique culture, and tradition. His country receives a huge number of tourist every year, the tourism industry has a great impact on the economy of his country. His country is famous for Mt. Everest, Gautam Buddha, Yeti, Gorkhali (World Bravest Army), highest lake, deepest gorge, and for many other reasons. He likes to refer this place to all the travelers who love to visit new places.

HOW TO USE THIS BOOK

The *Greater Than a Tourist* book series was written by someone who has lived in an area for over three months. The goal of this book is to help travelers either dream or experience different locations by providing opinions from a local. The author has made suggestions based on their own experiences. Please check before traveling to the area in case the suggested places are unavailable.

Travel Advisories: As a first step in planning any trip abroad, check the Travel Advisories for your intended destination.
https://travel.state.gov/content/travel/en/traveladvisories/traveladvisories.html

FROM THE PUBLISHER

Traveling can be one of the most important parts of a person's life. The anticipation and memories that you have are some of the best. As a publisher of the Greater Than a Tourist, as well as the popular *50 Things to Know* book series, we strive to help you learn about new places, spark your imagination, and inspire you. Wherever you are and whatever you do I wish you safe, fun, and inspiring travel.

Lisa Rusczyk Ed. D.
CZYK Publishing

WELCOME TO
> TOURIST

"Never go on trips with anyone
you do not love"

\- Ernest Hemingway

Hello everyone, this is the book for the one who is planning to visit Nepal. Nepal is a hot destination for every tourist across the world. Nepal receives a huge number of tourist every year and they are celebrating 'Visit Nepal 2020' intending to attract 2 million tourists. So, in this book, I have mentioned 50 tips and tricks plus two bonus tips which every tourist should read before traveling to Nepal. These 52 tips will help you to know more closely about Nepal. You will be familiar to the Nepalese culture, and tradition, you will know the top tourist destination places of Nepal, You will know the tips to roam with a limited budget, you will know the average price of accommodation and food, and actually, you will know everything related to Nepal.

Thus, in this book, you will find very informative content which will make you familiar with all the major stuff related to Nepal. This book will help you to travel in Nepal like a local, and this book will surely make you more excited about your next trip to Nepal. So, let's begin our 52 important tips and tricks about Nepal Tourism.

Nepal

Kathmandu
Nepal
Climate

	High	Low
January	65	38
February	71	42
March	77	48
April	83	55
May	84	61
June	84	67
July	83	69
August	84	68
September	82	65
October	79	57
November	73	47
December	67	40

GreaterThanaTourist.com

Temperatures are in Fahrenheit degrees.
Source: NOAA

As we all want to travel to different places in the world. We want to see every beautiful creation present on earth and Nepal is one of the hot destinations for all tourists. Tourists are attracting towards Nepal because of its unique culture and tradition, natural sceneries, artificial beauties, and for many other reasons. But before moving to Nepal, you need to know these 50 very important tips, and they are highlighted below:

1. MAINTAIN DISTANCE WHILE TALKING:

Nonverbal communications are different in different countries. Therefore, it is very important to learn non-verbal communication while traveling to other countries. So in the context of Nepal, you just need to maintain distance while talking to any Nepalese people. You should not go too close while communicating with them because they can't digest it. While talking to the local people always take care of the distance, be confident, and look into their eyes. Don't be shy and don't look here and there while communicating with the local people. It is their culture and habit to maintain some distance while communicating. So every tourist across the world should know about this fact.

2. DO NOT SMOKE IN PUBLIC PLACES:

Smoking a cigarette is common all over the world. Smoking a cigarette is also very common in Nepal. You get a pack of a cigarette in any grocery shop. But remember one thing that you are not allowed to smoke in public places like a bus, road, taxi, Taxi station, etc. You can smoke in your room, restaurant, and in a private place. If you caught smoking in the public places, then you may have to pay a certain amount of a fine to the government of Nepal. You should be responsible and should think about the health of other public people. And also if you are under 18 years of age, then it is illegal to smoke in Nepal.

3. DO NOT CARRY MARIJUANA/WEED:

Smoking marijuana is popular all over the world. Marijuana was legal in Nepal in the early 1800s to the 1970s. Many foreign people used to come to Nepal just to buy weed of Nepal. But from 1973, Nepal canceled the license of all shops who were selling marijuana due to the pressure of the United States of America and from the international community. Today Marijuana or weed is illegal in Nepal. There are strict rules for weed/marijuana. But in some state of the US and Canada, a weed is legal, and if you come here with the same thought, then you may fall into great trouble. So never carry weed or marijuana, and also other illegal drugs.

4. KISSING IN PUBLIC PLACES IS STRICTLY PROHIBITED:

In western countries kissing your loved one in public places is normal, but it is not allowed in

South Asian countries like Nepal, India, Pakistan, Srilanka, Bhutan, Bangladesh, Afghanistan, China, and the Maldives. Their cultures and traditions are different, they cannot digest this kind of activity. You must need to understand the culture and tradition of Nepalese people. So it is better to avoid kissing, touching, and coming closer in the public places.

5. PACK BOTH WINTER AND SUMMER CLOTHES:

Nepal has a wide variety of climates. If in some places in Nepal there is a hot climate, then in some places you can find a cool climate. You will be amazed seeing the climate of Nepal, you need to see weather report before traveling to any places in Nepal. Therefore, it is better to bring both summer and winter clothes while traveling to Nepal.

6. ALWAYS TRAVEL FROM ROADWAYS:

Always try to travel from roadways because it is cheaper than airways and you can explore different natural beauties of Nepal more closely. If you want to explore the beauties of Nepal without spending huge money, then it is better to travel from roadways. But if you don't want to compromise your comfort, then you can travel from the airways. If your budget is tight, then I suggest you travel from roadways. Airways is very expensive for a tourist in Nepal.

7. $35 PER DAY FOR EACH PERSON IS ENOUGH:

Nepal is one of the cheapest countries in the world. You can enjoy your day in Nepal with less than $35 per day. Hotel expenses, food expenses, tour expenses, everything can be covered within $35 if you use your money wisely. Don't buy the things which you won't use, try to bargain because they may price goods and services higher than the market price, and try to bring a student ID card if you are a student.

8. DON'T MISS TO VISIT PASHUPATINATH TEMPLE:

Pashupatinath Temple is one of the biggest temples of Lord Shiva. Every year thousands of tourists from all over the world visit here. You can see the tradition, the belief of Hindus people, you can see the different handmade architecture, statues, and many more things. But never use your camera inside the temple, because capturing photo is restricted here. One more thing I would like to add is that if you are from Western countries, African countries, then you are not allowed to enter inside the temple because only Hindu people are allowed to enter, it has very strict rules and policy. But there are lots of things outside to enjoy, and the best thing is that you can capture the photo.

9. CARRY A WATER BOTTLE:

While traveling to Nepal, you have to carry a water bottle. You can find free drinking water in most of the places; it will reduce your cost. A water bottle is not so expensive in Nepal compared to other western countries, but a small saving will surely benefit you; it will cover your other expenses. While staying at the hotel do not order a water bottle, it may cost you two times more expensive than the market rate. And one more thing, do not throw a plastic bottle anywhere, you just need to throw it in the dustbin; otherwise, you have to pay a certain fine to the municipality.

10. DO NOT HIRE A TAXI AFTER LANDING AT TRIBHUVAN INTERNATIONAL AIRPORT:

Taxis inside the Tribhuvan International Airport are so expensive. They may charge you a very high amount, hire no taxi inside the airport. I suggest you travel by foot because you can see the city more closely. But if the destination is too far, then it is better to book online cab. Uber and Ola are not available in Nepal, but you can book 'Sarathi'. Sarathi is a taxi app that will charge you a fair amount compared to other taxis, and they provide 24/7 services to their customers. Another better option is to use public transport; they are a lot cheaper than other services. You can also hire two-wheeler vehicles like motorbike and scooter. Tootle and Pathao are the leading company in Nepal, you can book motorbike or scooter from these companies, their fare rates are also cheap, and you can enjoy the view of the city more clearly.

11. EXPLORE THE KATHMANDU CITY FROM SWAMBHUNATH TEMPLE:

Swambhunath Temple is at the west of Kathmandu city, this temple is also known as the 'Monkey Temple'. This is the sacred place of Buddhist pilgrimage, but it is open for everyone. This temple is one of the oldest religious sites of Nepal which was founded at the beginning of the 5th century. You can see a fantastic design, architecture, stupa, and culture and tradition. You can see a large pair of eyes on each side of the main stupa which tries to represent wisdom and compassion. The temple is very tall, you need to climb stairs. But after reaching there, you can see an exquisite view of the whole Kathmandu city. You can see the view of the city by using binoculars too, but they will charge you a certain amount. The 2015 earthquake affected the temple, but now it is free of danger. There is no restriction of clicking photos, you can click photos everywhere. But I suggest you read the instruction because the rules might be updated. There are a lot of shops, restaurant, and cafe at

23

the downside of this temple, you can enjoy your quality time there as well.

12. EXPLORE DURBAR SQUARE, KATHMANDU:

Visit Durbar Square, Kathmandu, which is located at the former Kathmandu Kingdom Palace. Durbar Square shows the culture and history of the Kathmandu valley; the palace is decorated in Nepali culture and tradition. Durbar Square is also a UNESCO World Heritage Site, the earthquake of 2015 damaged it, but now it is free of danger. The palace has a museum, and it is also a home of Kumari (living Goddess). The best thing is that you can see this beautiful palace without paying any fee because the entry is free for everyone, and it is opened from early morning to night. Here is no restriction of clicking photos; you can capture your memory with no hesitation. So do not miss exploring this beautiful palace if you are in Kathmandu.

13. VISIT NARAYANHITI PALACE:

If you are interested in politics, then never miss visiting the Narayanhiti Palace which is situated in the Kathmandu Valley. It was a royal palace and after the introduction of democracy; it turned into a museum. Now it is opened for everyone, you can visit this palace to know the transformation of politics of Nepal. This palace also shows the lifestyle of Nepalese kings, their culture, and their environment. The royal massacre took place in this palace, blood, bullet holes are still visible. But capturing a photo inside the palace is strictly prohibited, you should not capture a photo of anything after entering inside the palace. The palace is closed on Tuesday and the rest of the day they open it from 11 am to 4 pm. Entry is not free, they charge a certain amount as an entry fee. Entry fee is different for different people. National people enter this palace at a low price, South Asian tourists pay higher than national people, and the rest of other tourists pay a little higher than a South Asian tourists. If you are a student, then don't forget to bring your student ID card, it will help you a lot to reduce your entry fee.

14. DON'T MISS VISITING GARDEN OF DREAMS:

Garden of Dreams is another famous tourist destination of Kathmandu. It is located in the Kaiser Mahal, at the entrance of Thamel. Garden of dreams is also known as 'Sapana ko Bagaicha' in Nepali. This garden was built in 1920, and it consists of 6,895 square meters, it has three pavilions, ponds, pergolas, urns, and an amphitheater. This beautiful garden was neglected by the Nepal government, but recently it is restored and financed by the Austrian government. This garden is open from 9 am to 10 pm, and the last entry is at 9 pm. Entry fee is not free; they charge you $4- $5 as an entry fee. This garden is a must-visit for every tourist who is in Kathmandu valley. Just go and enjoy this beautiful creation.

15. ENJOY STUNNING VIEWS FROM NAGARKOT:

Nagarkot is one of the top tourist destinations of Kathmandu; it gives you a pleasant view of Himalayas. Nagarkot is popular for its beautiful natural beauty; it has unique and attracting hotels. The view of this place is so breathtaking, and it has a very cool temperature. From Nagarkot, you can view Mount Everest and other eight peaks of Nepal. Many tourists visit this place just for a stunning view of world highest peak 'Mt. Everest'. You can also watch Kathmandu valley, Nambur forest, Rolwaling range, Ganesh Himal, Shivapuri National Park, and Langtang range. Once upon a time, this place was mainly used for monitoring other kingdoms, but now it is one of the famous hill stations of Nepal. This stunning place is located at the Bhaktapur district of the Kathmandu valley. The best time to visit this place is from October to March. The hotels of this place will be fully packed. So I suggest you book hotels before coming to this place.

16. VISIT HANUMAN DHOKA:

Hanuman Dhoka is a beautiful palace situated in the Kathmandu valley. It is a part of Durbar square; it was the palace of the Malla king, and shah dynasty. This palace covers 5 acres of land; the area of this palace is so big and beautiful. This palace was named after the Hindu lord Hanuman, we can see a standing statue of Hanuman at the entrance of this palace. The statue of standing hanuman is very old, it was built in 1672. The meaning of Hanuman Dhoka in English is 'Gate of Lord Hanuman'. This palace is located near to Durbar square, and the entrance is not free. They will charge 5 dollars for SAARC Nationals and $10 for other nationalities. There are a total of 8 countries in the SAARC, they are:

1. Nepal
2. India
3. Pakistan
4. Afghanistan
5. Srilanka
6. Bhutan
7. Maldives
8. Bangladesh.

17. SAY 'NAMASTE' WHILE GREETING NEPALESE PEOPLE:

If you want to impress local people of Nepal, then you must need to learn some basic local words. While meeting any Nepalese people on the go, you can say, Namaste or Namaskar to them; it simply means 'Hello'. Namaste is spoken by pressing hands together, by touching palms, by pointing fingers upward, and thumb must be close to the chest. Most of the people from urban areas are comfortable in speaking English, but when you go to rural areas of Nepal, you might feel difficult to communicate. So to impress them you can say Namaste, it helps to create a friendly environment and good relationship. Nepalese people will surely be happy; they will feel that their culture and tradition are admired by the whole world. So instead of saying 'Hello', it is better to greet them in their local language, they will appreciate it.

18. ROAM IN THE STREET OF THAMEL:

Thamel is a tourist hub of the Kathmandu valley. You can see tourists from different countries roaming in the street of Thamel. This place is generally popular for hotels, shops, restaurants, and cafes. By visiting this place, you can enjoy the nightlife. The prices of food in the hotels of Thamel are very expensive compared to other hotels in the Kathmandu valley, so if you are on a tight budget, be on your limit. Different programs and function are organized to enjoy the tourist. This is a commercial place which is also famous for buying different products of Nepal such as; khukuri, incense sticks, books, Pashmina shawl, Dhaka Topi, and so many other things. But always bargain a little because they may price you higher than the market rate. Entry to this place is completely free, there is no entry fee, you can visit this place at any time, and there is no time limit.

19. VISIT CASINO ROYALE:

Are you interested in playing cards and gambling? If your answer is yes, then you must need to visit this place. This place is located at Kathmandu valley which is one of the most popular casinos in the country, it is a very good place to hangout. It has a number of a table where you can enjoy playing different card games, gambling, and other plays. There is one offer for visitors, if you stay here for a long time by playing different games, then you can get an opportunity to enjoy dinner buffets. It is the best place where you can enjoy with your friends and family, and you will also be able to know about the casino culture of Nepal. Entry is free; you don't need to pay a single penny, but you may be charged a certain fee for playing games.

20. EXPLORE KUMARI BAHAL:

Have you heard about 'Living Goddess', if not, then you can see the living Goddess in this place. Kumari Devi is a living goddess of Nepal; Nepalese people worship her with great enthusiasm. Kumari Bahal is a home of a living Goddess which is a three-story courtyard. You can see Kumari, or living Goddess roaming inside the Kumari Bahal. It is very difficult to capture the living goddess in a lens, but if you visit Indra Jatra which is held every September, then you can see the living goddess of Nepal. This house of the living goddess can also be seen from Durbar Square. But one thing you must be clear that you are not allowed to capture photos as it is strictly prohibited. If you found capturing photos, then the concerned authority may punish you.

21. VISIT CENTRAL ZOO:

Are you an animal lover? Do you feel good while looking at different animals? Do you want to click a selfie with animals? If your answers are yes to all of these questions, then never miss visiting the central zoo, which is located at Jawalakhel, Lalitpur. You can see different wild animals, birds, mammals, reptiles, and so on. This zoo is a home of approximately 870 animals in 109 species. It was established in 1932 by Rana Prime Minister, originally it was a private zoo, and in 1956 it was opened for public people. You will also see different unique birds and animals that are found only in Nepal. One-horned rhinoceros, Asiatic elephant, marbled cat, etc are some attraction. Apart from animals, this zoo has a very good environment; there are several artificial attractions where you can capture your beautiful photo. It also has a library, a playground for children, picnic areas, a lake, and many more. Fishing on the lake may be allowed, but please confirm it before fishing; rules keep changing according to the time.

22. SEE THE REMAINS OF DHARAHARA:

Never miss a chance to see the remains of Dharahara, which is located at Sundhara, Kathmandu. Dharahara which was also known as Bhimsen tower was a 9-story tower, but it was destroyed by the 2015 earthquake, now only the base of this tower is present. Sixty dead bodies were found in the rubble, however, reconstruction of this tower has already been started. You can visit this place to see the power of 2015 earthquake, it also has very good restaurants and cafe where you can enjoy your quality time. The tower was unique; it was designed in Mughal, and European style, it had a spiral staircase with almost 213 steps. Dharahara was the tallest tower of Nepal which was built by Bhimsen Thapa for Queen Lalit Tripura Sundari. Now, it is under construction; it is said that it will be ready in 3 years, and it will be earthquake resistance. According to the concerned authority, the total expenses for reconstructing Dharahara is about 3 billion, it is said that it will be more beautiful, and more features will be added. Till then just see the remains of Dharahara and enjoy your quality time by drinking coffee in the nearby restaurant and cafe.

23. TRAVEL TO POKHARA:

After enjoying these beautiful places of Kathmandu, you should travel to Pokhara. Pokhara is a very beautiful city which is rich in its natural beauties, it is also considered as the tourism capital of Nepal. This beautiful city is 200 km west of Kathmandu. You can either travel from a tourist bus or an airplane, depending on your budget. Pokhara has 3 out of 10 highest mountains in the world i.e. Dhaulagiri, Annapurna, and Manaslu. The roadway from Kathmandu to Pokhara is little congested, and uncomfortable, but you can forget it by looking at beautiful natural beauties, you can see high mountains, lakes, and green environment on the go. In the street of Pokhara, you can see people from different countries, you will surely feel that the number of tourists are more than the local people. This place might be a little expensive, so you need to use your money wisely.

24. STAY IN THE LAKESIDE:

If you are coming to Pokhara just for enjoying your vacation, then never stay out of the lakeside, always stay in the lakeside hotel of Pokhara. Every attraction of Pokhara is present in a lakeside. Lakeside hotels will give you a very beautiful picture of nature, you can see stunning Phewa Lake, mountains, and so on. Every tourism activities are performed inside the lakeside area. You will see people boating on the Phewa Lake, you will see people paragliding, and you will have an opportunity to interact with different people of the world as every tourist stays in the lakeside hotels. Good hotels, cafes, restaurants, etc are present inside the lakeside, different programs, events, etc are performed inside the lakeside. The lakeside is a heaven of Pokhara, so it is better to stay in lakeside hotels if you are coming here for vacation. Price of a room is higher in a lakeside hotel comparing to the offside hotel, but I swear it's worth it. You will find every tourism service in the lakeside area.

25. VISIT PHEWA TAL (LAKE):

The first things to do in Pokhara is to visit Phewa Tal. Just dress up, come outside, and directly come to Phewa Tal. Phewa Tal is one of the top tourist destinations of Pokhara. It is the second largest lake of Nepal, which covers an area of 4.43 sq km, and it has an average depth of 8.6 m. It is stunning; it has very clear and freshwater, and the views of this lake will surely hold your breath. The best time to visit this lake is early in the morning, you can enjoy your cup of coffee or tea just sitting near to this lake. There is a temple called Taal Barahi in the middle of this lake, and to go there you need to book a boat, the fare of the boat is not expensive, and you can go by sharing as well. Taal Barahi is the Hindu temple, don't miss it, visit this beautiful temple, you will have an opportunity to know the culture of Nepalese people. You can see different beautiful fishes on the lake, as water is visible, but never try to do fishing, it is strictly prohibited.

26. VISIT RUPA TAL:

Another stunning place of Pokhara is Rupa Tal (Lake). If you want to enjoy freshwater, if you want to do fishing, and if you want to do boating, then you must have to come to Rupa Tal. Rupa Tal is the third-largest Tal of Pokhara valley, and it is situated in the south-east of Pokhara valley. You will have a chance to enjoy a fresh environment of Rupa Tal. Till now 36 species of water birds are recorded in the lake and it is 19% of the total 193 wetland-dependent birds found in Nepal. If you love eating fresh fish, then the management of Rupa Tal is also doing the business of Fish. Entry to this place is free; however, you may charge for doing boating, fishing, and other activities.

27. VISIT SARANGKOT:

Sarangkot is one of the top destination places of Pokhara, and it lies on the outskirts of Pokhara city. To enjoy in Sarangkot, you need to travel early in the morning. You should leave for Sarangkot at 4:00 am so that you can see a clear view of the sunrise. It gives you a very pleasant view of nature, you can also see the stunning view of the Annapurna Himalayan Range, and it also allows you to view the orange hues with some very beautiful mountain ranges. You will not be alone traveling Sarangkot at early in the morning, you can see huge public traveling to Sarangkot at early in the morning to experience such a beauty of nature. But if you feel difficulty to wake up and travel at 4:00 am, then you can stay at Sarangkot for 1 day, there are also several budget hotels and homestay. Sarangkot is also famous for paragliding if you are a fan of paragliding then pack your bags and visit directly to Sarangkot. You will experience the real pleasure of paragliding. The best time to visit this place is from October to January.

28. VISIT GORKHA MEMORIAL MUSEUM:

You might have heard about Gorkha, and if you haven't heard then let me tell you. Gorkha is the bravest army of the world. England, India, Singapore, and many other countries recruit Gorkha every year. Gorkha troops belong to Nepal, so in this museum, you will find every detail about the Gorkha troops. It is located at lamachaur road, Pokhara. This museum talks about the bravery of Gorkhali. The uniform of brave Gorkha troops are presented there. Visitors can also have a chance to view medals, gifts, awards, sword, etc of late Gorkha troops. This museum is open from 8:30 am to 4:30 pm and the entry is not free, they may charge 100-200 Nepalese rupees as an entry fee. You also need to pay a camera fee if you have brought a camera with you.

29. ENJOY IN DAVI'S FALL:

If you are in Pokhara, then you should not miss this amazing place. It is the famous tourist destination of Pokhara. You will see beautiful and a stunning view of a waterfall. This place is named Devi's fall because, on 31 July 1961, Swiss couple named Davi was swimming in this place, but women drowned and her body was found after 3 days. Her father wished to name it as a Davi's fall, and after that, this place name was converted to Davi's fall. The Nepali name of this beautiful place is Patale Chango. Entry is no free; they may charge you $1-$2 as an entry fee. The best time to visit this place is a monsoon, you can see the heavy waterfall, and you can also clearly hear the strong sound of water. In this place, you can also try your luck on the luck pond. To be lucky, you need to throw coins in the pond and that coin must be placed on the statue of God.

30. VISIT THE ANNAPURNA BUTTERFLY MUSEUM:

If you love watching a butterfly, if you love catching butterflies, then Nepal is the best place to witness some exciting butterflies. The best place to see butterflies in Pokhara is the Annapurna Butterfly Museum. This amazing butterfly museum is located near to Prithvi Narayan Campus, Bagartole. Here you can see different, unique, beautiful, and exciting butterflies of Nepal. This museum will give you detailed knowledge about Nepalese butterflies. Every moment spent on this museum will give you great pleasure. Don't miss the chance to see Corman Birding which is regarded as the largest butterfly of Nepal. It is a small museum, and it does not charge any fee. Entry is free; however, it may change its policy in the future. The best time to visit this place is post-monsoon, you will see huge tourists at that time.

31. TRAVEL TO CHITWAN:

Chitwan is another top tourist spot of Nepal which is located in the southwestern part of Province no 3 which has an area of 2238.29 sq km. It is located in the Terai region, and the climate of this place might be hot. Chitwan has a variety of flora and fauna, and the first national park of Nepal called Chitwan National Park is located here. You can see a variety of lakes and rivers, you can also experience Narayani River, which flows north to south in the west of Bharatpur. Narayani River is the deepest and one of the biggest rivers in Nepal. Chitwan is also famous for a picnic spot, every year, thousands of internal and external tourist visit Chitwan just to enjoy their picnic. Places like Das Dhunga, Bazaari Tal attract a huge number of tourists every year. Trekking, bird watching, Bungee jumping, jungle safari, and watching elephant games are major activities which every tourist need to experience. You can find good hotels, restaurants, and cafe in a budget, so pack your bags and move towards Chitwan.

32. VISIT CHITWAN NATIONAL PARK:

The first thing to do in Chitwan is to visit Chitwan National Park. Chitwan National park is the first national park of Nepal which was established in 1973, and it got the status of the world heritage site in 1984. It covers an area of 952.63 sq km which is a home of several animals. You can see different unique, and endangered animals. It has 68 species of mammals and 543 species of birds. Bengal tiger, leopard, Bengal foxes, spotted linsangs, one-horned rhinoceros, fishing cat, golden jackals, jungle cats, etc are some attraction of this place. You can also enjoy watching birds in this national park. Kingfisher, crowned Prinia, jungle fowl, eastern imperial eagle, oriental darter, etc are some unique birds which are found in this national park. In this national park, you can go to jungle safari, you can go fishing, you can enjoy watching birds, and you can see different vegetation. Entry is not free, you need to pay a fee for entering into this beautiful park.

33. GO TO CHITWAN THARU VILLAGE:

Another thing to do in Chitwan is to go to the Chitwan Tharu Village. If you love watching, learning, and experiencing the cultures of Nepal, then it is better to go to the Chitwan Tharu Village. You will get an opportunity to learn the unique, and exciting culture of the Tharu people. You can learn the daily life of the Tharu people. You can walk, and can also take a Tonka ride to explore Tharu museum and old traditional houses. Tharu museum helps you to provide more detail information about the Tharu community. It is a very good place to enjoy your quality time, they perform their cultural dance, sing their cultural songs, and provide cultural foods. Going Chitwan Tharu village is a top thing to do in Chitwan which no one should miss. Enjoy your quality time with the local people, and learn some good culture.

34. CANOEING IN NARAYANI RIVER:

Narayani River is the deepest river of Nepal, and it is also one of the largest rivers of Nepal. If you love canoeing then this place is for you. Canoeing is a very popular thing to do in Narayani River. You will get an opportunity to do canoeing in the deepest river of Nepal, where you can also explore the Chitwan National park. You will get an opportunity to see various animals of Chitwan National Park while doing canoeing in Narayani River. Boating service is also available in Narayani River, you can snap a picture of crocodiles, birds, and the beautiful environment. And another good thing is that from September 2019 cruise service will also start where the tourist can explore the river more closely and comfortably. Entry is free, but you will have to pay for doing boating, canoeing, and rafting. Fishing on this river is allowed, but confirm it from the concerned authority because rules and policies might change according to the time.

35. ENJOY ELEPHANT SAFARI:

An Elephant Safari is the most exciting activities which every tourist need to enjoy. Elephant safari will give you a stunning view of the whole National park, you can enjoy wild creatures of National park more closely which includes one-horned rhinoceros, Royal Bengal Tiger, and also different types of winged animals and number of reptiles. You can capture a photo of several different endangered animals, and you can film it too. There is no restriction to click photos. Elephant safari will guarantee to add fun and excitement in your tour, try it once if you are in Chitwan. However, it is not free, they will charge some amount, but I swear it worth it. If you are afraid of riding elephant then don't worry, you can enjoy doing jeep safari too. But I suggest you go for Elephant Safari, it is unique, and much more exciting than a jeep safari.

36. EXPLORE ELEPHANT BREEDING CENTER:

Never miss visiting elephant breeding center if you are in Chitwan. An elephant is the most beautiful animal found on the earth. If you love watching the elephant, if you want to know details about the elephant, then this center is for you. You will get a huge opportunity to explore reproducing focus. In elephant breeding centers, you will see how elephant meals are prepared, how they eat it, and you will also learn about the nature and habits of elephants. This center was established in 1985 to protect endangered elephants in the region. There are several baby elephants and a small museum too. The place is walkable, if you enjoy walking, then don't go to a rickshaw or any vehicles. It will only take 40-50 minutes to reach this center. The elephant breeding center is open from 6 am to 6 pm, but reach before 4 pm so that you can take your time to explore this beautiful center. Entry is not free, and the fee structure is different for different tourists. For internal tourists, they charge Rs 25, Rs 50 for SAARC nation tourists, and Rs 100 for western tourists. If you are a student, then don't forget to bring an ID card; you may get a discount.

37. ENJOY ELEPHANT BATHING:

Another exciting thing to do in Chitwan is to enjoy showering and swimming with elephants in Rapti River. Elephant bathing will give you great fun; you will enjoy bathing with an elephant in profound water of Rapti streams. It's your choice, you can jump or plunge into the Rapti River according to your desire. You can play with this beautiful animal and you can dive in the river from the back of the elephant while it is bathing. There is also a virtual competition between several tourists to capture the photographs of a bathing elephant. You can also purchase a ticket to bathe an elephant in the Rapti River from various guest houses and travel agencies. The cost of the ticket will fall between 200-600 Nepalese rupees. But if you don't want to spend money on that then just go to Rapti River at evening where elephant riders come to bathe their elephant, enjoy this beautiful moment for free.

38. VISIT THE CROCODILE BREEDING CENTER:

Don't miss visiting this beautiful center if you are in Chitwan. The Crocodile reproducing focus is another most interesting program which you can explore in Crocodile Breeding Center. It is located in Kasara, of Chitwan National Park. This breeding center protects and conserves endangered genetic crocodiles such as Gharials or Mugars. Eggs of crocodiles are hatched in this breeding center and it is released in the rivers of Nepal. You will get detailed information related to crocodiles, you will be able to understand the nature and habit of crocodiles. To travel to this center, you need to book a private jeep/car or you can ask your hotel to manage it because there is no regular transportation. Entry is not free; you have to pay an entrance fee to Chitwan National Park, and after that, you have to pay an entrance fee for this center.

39. ENJOY SLEEPING IN THE TOWER OF CHITWAN NATIONAL PARK:

Do you want to spend your nights along with other wild animals? If your answer is yes, then let me tell you that there is a tower in the Chitwan National Park where you can spend a couple of nights which will help you to explore the behavior of wild animals. You will get an opportunity to spend your whole night in the middle of the Chitwan jungle where you can experience sunrise and sunset inside the jungle. There is a basic toilet inside the tower because wild animals will be aggressive if they see a human being roaming in the jungle. You should not come outside of your tower, just remain inside, and explore from inside. To spend a night in the tower inside the Chitwan jungle needs huge guts, if you are a weak-hearted person, then you should not try this. You will have to pay a certain amount for spending a night here, it is not so expensive, go for it if you are excited.

40. WATCH ELEPHANT GAMES SHOWS:

Chitwan is also famous for the elephant games shows. Chitwan host several adventurous and entertaining game shows. Never miss seeing these beautiful games shows because it is unique and very exciting. Most famous games shows watched by many people are elephant race, elephant polo, elephant football, elephant beauty contest, picnic, elephant dramas, and elephant hockey. But these games are not operated regularly; they are organized on some favorable season or a yearly basis. Entry is not free; you will need to pay an entry fee to experience these entertaining games shows. Don't miss this beautiful opportunity; it will add beautiful memory to your list. Capture this moment or film this moment because this moment may not occur several times in the life of people.

41. VISIT MUSTANG:

After traveling to Chitwan, you need to go directly to Mustang. Mustang is a heaven on earth, In fact, it is the most beautiful place in Nepal. It is a last district of Nepal and has an area of 3573 sq km. Mustang is the least populated district of Nepal; it has approximately 14000 population. It is the wealthy district of Nepal with a GDP per capita of $2466.The headquarter of this beautiful place is Jomsom. The environment of this place is so eye-catching. High mountains, different beautiful caves, clear sky, attractive and unique hotels, fresh environment, and many other things will surely blow your mind. If you won't visit this beautiful place, then you will never see the real beauty of Nepal. Mustang is a little expensive than other places because it is located in the offside area, so the price of products is a little higher than the actual market price. Explore this heaven of the earth if you are in Nepal.

42. VISIT MUKTINATH TEMPLE:

Muktinath temple is one of the most popular temples among the Hindus and Buddhist people of the world. This is a Vishnu temple which is located in the Muktinath valley, Mustang. Muktinath temple is one of the highest temples in the world, which is at an altitude of 3800m. This temple is also known as Mukti Kshetra, which means the place of liberation. Every year, thousands of a tourist visit this unique, and most beautiful temple, and every person is allowed to explore this temple. You don't need to be Hindu or Buddhist to visit this temple. There is a tap in Muktinath temple, and it is said that any people who bath in that tap his/her sin will be washed away. Most of the people bath in that tap to wash their sin. So visit this temple and explore the culture and tradition of Nepalese people.

43. VISIT MARPHA:

Marpha is a beautiful place located in the Mustang District. It is a village development committee which has a very low population. According to the census of 1991, there were only 1630 people who were living in 434 individual households. The meaning of 'Marpha' in English is hardworking people. Tourism is the main means of survival of the people of this place. This village is rich in the production of an apple, it is also known as the apple capital of Nepal. Marpha Brandy, jams, local alcohol, etc are prepared from this local fruit. This place is less crowded, as there is no huge population. Many tourists come to this place by doing trekking. Tourist is attracted in this place to see the quiet environment, unique hotels, and motels, and the main reason is to taste local fruit. They taste the local jam, Marpha brandy, local alcohols, and many other things. They also buy fresh local fruits and other products to take back to their home as a memory.

44. EXPLORE JOMSOM:

Jomsom is the headquarters of the Mustang District. You can travel to Jomsom by booking flight to Kathmandu–Pokhara, and then after Pokhara–Jomsom. There is no direct flight from Kathmandu to Jomsom. But let me tell you that the airport of Jomsom falls under the world dangerous airport, the airport is very breathtaking. But the well qualified and experienced pilots will take you to Jomsom very comfortably. Jomsom is situated at an altitude of 2700m; the place is covered with huge mountains. Jomsom is famous for trekking, every year's more than 30000 tourists from all over the world trek in Jomsom, it helps them to reveal the Nepal Spectacular diversity. The trekkers will able to see deep valleys, high mountains, a wide range of people and terrain, dry landscape, beautiful hotels and motels, and many other things. Apart from trekking, you can also do jeep safari to view the real beauty of Jomsom. But if you love trekking, then it is better to trek because you will be able to view the beauties of Jomsom more closely.

45. OTHER MAIN ATTRACTIONS OF MUSTANG:

We can't list every beautiful place of Mustang because if we do so, then other beautiful places of Nepal may not get a chance. There are a lot more things to do in Mustang. Mustang is a heaven on earth. I am 100% sure that the beauty of this place will remain in your heart for the rest of your life. Some other major things to do in Mustang are listed below:

1. Travel to Jhong Village
2. Travel to Jharkot Village
3. Visit Devthen Chhorten
4. Explore Lhungfu Cave
5. Visit Frigid spots to enjoy the snowfall
6. Enjoy bike tour in the Himalayas
7. Participate in Festival ceremony and adventure sports
8. Visit Chhairo Monastery
9. Visit Royal Palace of Mustang
10. Explore Red Monastery

46. TRAVEL TO PROVINCE 1:

After completing your tour of Mustang travel to province number 1. Province number 1 has very beautiful and eye-catching natural beauty. The flow of tourists to these places is very low because of the lack of promotion and advertisement. But the state government is working hard to promote its place in the world. The world's highest peak, Mt. Everest lies in this state. Province number 1 has a huge potential for attracting thousands of tourists, and every year the number of tourists traveling to this place is slowly growing. Places like Vedetar, Namaste Jharna, Illam, Fikkal, Kanyam, Dharan, etc are the major tourist destination of this state. Tea garden, waterfall, zoo, high mountains, the highest peak of the world, fresh environment, are some attraction of Province number 1. Hire a jeep or you can travel by public transportation to the tourist destination of Province 1. Roads are blacktopped, there are good hotels and motels, just pack your bags and carry your camera to experience the beauty of Province number 1.

47. VISIT VEDETAR:

Vedetar is a village development committee of Dhankutta district. It is situated in eastern Nepal, province number 1. To visit Vedetar, first you need to travel Biratnagar, it is a Capital of Province 1. Vedetar is only 62.4 km far from Biratnagar, hire a jeep or travel by public transportation. Vedetar is 1420 meters high from the sea level. It is a very cool place; it has a good cafe and hotels, and you can relax and chill out with your friends. It has a tower from where you can see a stunning view of the whole vedetar. The entry fee will be charged, which may cost you $1. Beautiful Pathivara Temple is also located in the Vedetar, you need to walk for 20 minutes to reach this temple. The road is graveled, but the view from that road is very beautiful. Walk for 20 minutes to visit this temple and experience the culture and tradition of Nepalese people.

48. EXPLORE NAMASTE JHARNA:

Namaste Jharna is located straight to Vedetar. It is a very attractive place where hundreds of internal and Indians tourists visit per day to enjoy in the water. Due to a lack of advertisement and promotion, this place is unable to attract external tourists. Only a few foreign tourists are seen in this beautiful waterfall. Due to the open border to India, we can see a huge number of Indians tourists. The view of the waterfall is very beautiful, falls is about 80m high, and it is in the shape of Namaste. This place is also visited by different researchers to research about the mountains, waterfall, vegetation, and many more things. Entry to this place is not free; it may charge approximately 50 Nepalese rupees. There is good management of hotels and a cafe.

49. VISIT ILLAM:

Illam district is one of the most beautiful districts of Nepal which is located in the province No. 1 of eastern Nepal. This district covers an area of 1703 sq km which has 290254 population. Illam is famous for a tea garden; the tea of Illam is exported to different parts of the world. It attracts different researchers to research rare birds, red panda, and other endangered animals. Illam is famous for pilgrimage tourism. Devi temples, Gajurmukhi, and other religious spots attract thousands of tourists every year. Illam is also famous for 9-cornered Mai Pokhari Lake, which is also known as the abode of the goddess. Mane pass connects Illam with Darjeeling district, India. The place is not expensive compared to other tourist destinations; you may spend $70 to $80 per week for accommodation and food. Don't miss your chance to explore natural and artificial beauties of Province No. 1.

50. EXPLORE MOUNT EVEREST WITH YOUR NAKED EYES:

Mount Everest is the highest peak in the world which is located in Province No. 1, Nepal. The height of Mt. Everest is 8848 m, however, it is old data, and a new height of Mount Everest will be public soon because it is in the process of calculation. Every year a huge number of tourists from all over the world come to Nepal to view and climb this world's highest peak. Nepal generates huge money because of Mount Everest. Tourist needs to pay a royalty to the Nepal government to climb this highest mountain. Tenzing Norgay Sherpa and Edmund Hillary were the people who climbed Mount Everest for the first time. There is good management of hotels, cafes, restaurants, and homestay. To reach Mount Everest or Everest Base Camp, there is a direct flight from Kathmandu to Lukla. If you are a fan of trekking, then start your trek from Lukla to Everest base camp; otherwise, you can take flight. But I suggest doing trekking because you will be able to see Sherpa village, Namche Bazaar, Sagarmatha National Park, and other natural beauties on the way. After 10-12 days of trekking, you will reach Everest Base Camp. Pack your bags and be ready for most exciting and adventurous trekking from Lukla to Everest or Everest Base Camp.

BONUS TIP 1. FOODS TO EAT IN NEPAL:

While traveling to Nepal, it is better to try or taste local food. There are several foods in Nepal that are popular all over the world. The local foods of Nepal are very tasty, and delicious. Some major foods of Nepal which you should not miss to taste are highlighted below:

1. Daal Bhaat
2. Momo
3. Chatamari
4. Dheedo
5. Sel Roti
6. Juju Dhau
7. Gundruk
8. Yomari
9. Bara
10. Choilaa

BONUS TIP 2. OTHER BEAUTIFUL PLACES OF NEPAL:

There are several other beautiful places in Nepal that should not be missed. Nepal is full of natural attractions; it is rich in its culture and tradition. So there are a lot of beautiful places in Nepal that we can't count in our hands. Some other very attractive places in Nepal are highlighted below:

1. Visit Janakpur to see the beautiful Janaki temple
2. Visit Koshi Tappu Wildlife Reserve, which is close to Kamladi, Kathmandu
3. Visit Lumbini, the birthplace of Gautam Buddha
4. Visit Asan, which is located in Kathmandu, Nepal
5. Visit Dharan to view high hills and fresh environment
6. Visit Bindyabasini temple, which is located in the Pokhara
7. Explore Parsa Wildlife Reserve, which is located in the Terai of Nepal

8. Visit Begnas Tal, which is located in the Pokhara for boating, fishing, and swimming.
9. Visit White Monastery, which is located in the Kathmandu valley
10. Explore Tilicho Lake, which is the highest lake in the world, located in the Manang region of Nepal.

Therefore, above 52 travel tips must be followed by every tourist to roam like a local in Nepal. Nepal is a beautiful place to visit; it is safe, affordable, and full of natural beauties. Nepal is also celebrating 'Visit Nepal 2020' intending to attract two million tourists. A tourist who lands first in the Tribhuvan International Airport will get several special travel benefits. Let's celebrate 'Visit Nepal 2020' and make it successful.

TOP REASONS TO BOOK THIS TRIP:

So you may be in confusion whether you need to travel to Nepal or not. So here are my top reasons to book this trip:

1. To explore the beauty of Mount Everest with your naked eyes
2. To visit the birthplace of Gautam Buddha
3. To explore different world heritage site
4. It is affordable and safe
5. To learn the culture and tradition of Nepalese People

OTHER RESOURCES:

1. https://www.welcomenepal.com/

2. https://www.tripadvisor.com/

3. http://www.tourism.gov.np/

PACKING AND PLANNING TIPS

A Week before Leaving

- Arrange for someone to take care of pets and water plants.

- Email and Print important Documents.

- Get Visa and vaccines if needed.

- Check for travel warnings.

- Stop mail and newspaper.

- Notify Credit Card companies where you are going.

- Passports and photo identification is up to date.

- Pay bills.

- Copy important items and download travel Apps.

- Start collecting small bills for tips.

- Have post office hold mail while you are away.

- Check weather for the week.

- Car inspected, oil is changed, and tires have the correct pressure.

- Check airline luggage restrictions.

- Download Apps needed for your trip.

Right Before Leaving

- Contact bank and credit cards to tell them your location.

- Clean out refrigerator.

- Empty garbage cans.

- Lock windows.

- Make sure you have the proper identification with you.

- Bring cash for tips.

- Remember travel documents.

- Lock door behind you.

- Remember wallet.

- Unplug items in house and pack chargers.

- Change your thermostat settings.

- Charge electronics, and prepare camera memory cards.

READ OTHER
GREATER THAN A TOURIST
BOOKS

Greater Than a Tourist- Geneva Switzerland: 50 Travel Tips from a Local by Amalia Kartika

Greater Than a Tourist- St. Croix US Birgin Islands USA: 50 Travel Tips from a Local by Tracy Birdsall

Greater Than a Tourist- San Juan Puerto Rico: 50 Travel Tips from a Local by Melissa Tait

Greater Than a Tourist – Lake George Area New York USA: 50 Travel Tips from a Local by Janine Hirschklau

Greater Than a Tourist – Monterey California United States: 50 Travel Tips from a Local by Katie Begley

Greater Than a Tourist – Chanai Crete Greece: 50 Travel Tips from a Local by Dimitra Papagrigoraki

Greater Than a Tourist – The Garden Route Western Cape Province South Africa: 50 Travel Tips from a Local by Li-Anne McGregor van Aardt

Greater Than a Tourist – Sevilla Andalusia Spain: 50 Travel Tips from a Local by Gabi Gazon

Children's Book: *Charlie the Cavalier Travels the World* by Lisa Rusczyk

73

> TOURIST

Follow us on Instagram for beautiful travel images:
http://Instagram.com/GreaterThanATourist

Follow *Greater Than a Tourist* on Amazon.

> TOURIST

At *Greater Than a Tourist*, we love to share travel tips with you. How did we do? What guidance do you have for how we can give you better advice for your next trip? Please send your feedback to GreaterThanaTourist@gmail.com as we continue to improve the series. We appreciate your constructive feedback. Thank you.

METRIC CONVERSIONS

TEMPERATURE

110° F —
100° F —   — 40° C
90° F —
80° F —   — 30° C
70° F —   — 20° C
60° F —
50° F —   — 10° C
40° F —
32° F —   — 0° C
20° F —
10° F —   — -10° C
0° F —
-10° F —   — -18° C
-20° F —   — -30° C

To convert F to C:

Subtract 32, and then multiply by 5/9 or .5555.

To Convert C to F:

Multiply by 1.8 and then add 32.

32F = 0C

LIQUID VOLUME

To Convert:..................Multiply by
U.S. Gallons to Liters................ 3.8
U.S. Liters to Gallons 26
Imperial Gallons to U.S. Gallons 1.2
Imperial Gallons to Liters....... 4.55
Liters to Imperial Gallons 22
1 Liter = .26 U.S. Gallon
1 U.S. Gallon = 3.8 Liters

DISTANCE

To convert ....Multiply by
Inches to Centimeters 2.54
Centimeters to Inches 39
Feet to Meters...................... .3
Meters to Feet 3.28
Yards to Meters 91
Meters to Yards 1.09
Miles to Kilometers 1.61
Kilometers to Miles............ .62
1 Mile = 1.6 km
1 km = .62 Miles

WEIGHT

1 Ounce = .28 Grams
1 Pound = .4555 Kilograms
1 Gram = .04 Ounce
1 Kilogram = 2.2 Pounds

TRAVEL QUESTIONS

- Do you bring presents home to family or friends after a vacation?

- Do you get motion sick?

- Do you have a favorite billboard?

- Do you know what to do if there is a flat tire?

- Do you like a sun roof open?

- Do you like to eat in the car?

- Do you like to wear sun glasses in the car?

- Do you like toppings on your ice cream?

- Do you use public bathrooms?

- Did you bring your cell phone and does it have power?

- Do you have a form of identification with you?

- Have you ever been pulled over by a cop?

- Have you ever given money to a stranger on a road trip?

- Have you ever taken a road trip with animals?

- Have you ever went on a vacation alone?

- Have you ever run out of gas?

- If you could move to any place in the world, where would it be?

- If you could travel anywhere in the world, where would you travel?

- If you could travel in any vehicle, which one would it be?

- If you had three things to wish for from a magic genie, what would they be?

- If you have a driver's license, how many times did it take you to pass the test?

- What are you the most afraid of on vacation?

- What do you want to get away from the most when you are on vacation?

- What foods smells bad to you?

- What item do you bring on ever trip with you away from home?

- What makes you sleepy?

- What song would you love to hear on the radio when you're cruising on the highway?

- What travel job would you want the least?

- What will you miss most while you are away from home?

- What is something you always wanted to try?

- What is the best road side attraction that you ever saw?

- What is the farthest distance you ever biked?

- What is the farthest distance you ever walked?

- What is the weirdest thing you needed to buy while on vacation?

- What is your favorite candy?

- What is your favorite color car?

- What is your favorite family vacation?

- What is your favorite food?

- What is your favorite gas station drink or food?

- What is your favorite license plate design?

- What is your favorite restaurant?

- What is your favorite smell?

- What is your favorite song?

- What is your favorite sound that nature makes?

- What is your favorite thing to bring home from a vacation?

- What is your favorite vacation with friends?

- What is your favorite way to relax?

- Where is the farthest place you ever traveled in a car?

- Where is the farthest place you ever went North, South, East and West?

- Where is your favorite place in the world?

- Who is your favorite singer?

- Who taught you how to drive?

- Who will you miss the most while you are away?

- Who if the first person you will contact when you get to your destination?

- Who brought you on your first vacation?

- Who likes to travel the most in your life?

- Would you rather be hot or cold?

- Would you rather drive above, below, or at the speed limited?

- Would you rather drive on a highway or a back road?

- Would you rather go on a train or a boat?

- Would you rather go to the beach or the woods?

TRAVEL BUCKET LIST

1.

2.

3.

4.

5.

6.

7.

8.

9.

10.

NOTES